Mildred,

Thank you for supporting me. God bless you now and always!

Love you and many thanks!

Always,
KoKo

Inspirational Collection

MONICA PETERSON

authorHOUSE

AuthorHouse™
1663 Liberty Drive
Bloomington, IN 47403
www.authorhouse.com
Phone: 833-262-8899

© 2021 Monica Peterson. All rights reserved.

No part of this book may be reproduced, stored in a retrieval system, or transmitted by any means without the written permission of the author.

Published by AuthorHouse 01/26/2022

ISBN: 978-1-6655-4840-3 (sc)
ISBN: 978-1-6655-4839-7 (e)

Print information available on the last page.

Any people depicted in stock imagery provided by Getty Images are models, and such images are being used for illustrative purposes only.
Certain stock imagery © Getty Images.

This book is printed on acid-free paper.

Because of the dynamic nature of the Internet, any web addresses or links contained in this book may have changed since publication and may no longer be valid. The views expressed in this work are solely those of the author and do not necessarily reflect the views of the publisher, and the publisher hereby disclaims any responsibility for them.

Contents

Dedication Page ix
Introduction xi

A Faithful God 1
Zig Zag 2
God's Promises 3
Everlasting Love 4
Your Provider 5
What Hatred Cannot Do 6
Turned Upside Down 7
True North 8
Touched By Life 9
The Most Important Words 10
The Grip of Grace 11
Standing on Faith 12
Slipping Away 13
Show and Tell 14
Stop, Drop and Roll 15
Saving Grace 16
Precious in His Sight 17
Praising You 18
Peace 19
My Prayer for You 20
It Could Have Been Me 21

If	22
I Choose You	23
I Am Enough	24
God's Word	25
Down on My Knees	26
Choices	27
Can You Hear Me?	28
Be with Me	29
A Plea for Mercy	30
A Living Sacrifice	31
A Grateful Heart	32
A Giving God	33
Without My Permission	34
War is Hell	35
Use Me Wisely	36
True Lies	37
The Ties That Bind	38
The Sinful Struggle	39
The Measure of A Man	40
The Essence of You	41
Technology	42
Silent Cries	43
Remember When?	45
Reflections of A Wife	46
Picking Up The Pieces	47
Optimism	49
Numb	50
Love to My Father	51
Life Stories	52
I Am Tired	53
From The Inside Out	54
Facets of Depression	55
Coronavirus Blues	56
Bent But Not Broken	57

Acceptance	59
A Purposeful Birth	60
A Blessing Born Out of Adversity	62
Will You Think of Me?	63
When My Life Is Over	64
The Whisper	66
Take Your Rest	67
Season of Grief	68
Room 301	69
Reflections	71
Missing You	72
Letting Go	73
I Can't Breathe	74
Fulfilling Your Destiny	75
Forever in My Heart	76
I Am, Because He Is	77
Love's Greatest Act	78
Learn To Listen	79
Senses	80
We Are Protected	81
Peaceful Existence	82
What Can We Render?	83
A Beautiful Surprise	84
TAKE ME AWAY	85
It's in the Blood	86
Feelings	87
About The Author	89

Dedication Page

This book is dedicated to my Lord and Savior, who REALLY is a God of second chances. Without His grace, mercy, unending love and forgiveness, none of this would be possible.

To Dwayne, thank you for believing in the words I put on paper and never doubting my ability. Thank you for enduring a few sleepless nights of reading, re-reading, and giving sometimes unwanted constructive criticism. Without your love and support this would not have been so much fun! I love you!

To my dad, Mr. David Loyd, an avid reader, who by example, taught me the joy of reading and soaking up knowledge in many different genres of books. My love for you is endless.

To Shelia Walker, you are the best big sister anyone could ask for. Thank you for always encouraging me in your own "unique" way. Words can never describe the love that I hold in my heart for you. (BKB forever!! 😊) Thank you Phillip!

To Mother Mary Marchand, you are too good to be true, I love you!

To Anita Owusu, thank you for always being there for me when I needed a listening ear. I love you. (BKB forever!! 😊)

Many thanks to William Moore. Your help was invaluable in navigating through this process. Love you so much!

To Rev. Fritzthadus Mack, your time and patience in making phone calls and offering spiritual guidance was invaluable and it meant more to me than you will ever know. Thank you, you are my friend for life!! Much love to you.

Last but certainly not least, to my late mother, Hazel, thank you for giving me life and for loving me without limitations. You will forever live in my heart and soul. I miss you more today than I did yesterday, until we meet again……

To the entire LOYD family, I love you all, without end!!

A sincere "thank you" to everyone who bought this book and was blessed by its contents!

Introduction

I offer these poems to each of you reading them in the hope that they will touch a piece of your soul.

I labored many nights and second-guessed myself, thinking that what I had to say was not important enough to be read, but after listening to the positive feedback I received and remembering that God did not give me a spirit of fear, but one of love, power, and a sound mind, in the end I decided to allow my faith to be bigger than my fear. I pray that in some way these words will be a blessing to someone.

The writings that are contained within this book were all inspired and given to me by God. It is my prayer that the words in this book will bless and uplift anyone who may be going through something that they feel no one else can understand. No matter where you are in life, at this very moment, God can and will see you through, if you just trust Him.

Shoot for the Stars!

Sincerely,
Monica Peterson

A Faithful God

I am surrounded on every hand but with God's help, I know I can stand.
As I look around me all I can see are faceless figures looking to devour me.
My soul cries out to God to protect me, please God,
keep me from the snares of the enemy.
The road to salvation seems long and hard,
but God has my back, for He is my guard.
When my enemies encamp me, my very soul they seek to steal,
the God that I serve is faithful, all I have to do is kneel.
When others try to do me harm, my faith stands on nothing less
than knowing that God is a shelter in the time of a storm.
My soul pleads for God's mercy and grace to give me strength to finish this race.
I love the Lord because He heard my cry, for when I am down to nothing,
He is always up to something that He will use for my good, there is never a need to ask why.
He loves me more than I could ever comprehend. He sticks closer than a brother,
He is my friend.
God never promised us a life that would be easy or one that would always be fun.
So, as I continue moving forward, I must turn my face to the SON!

Zig Zag

I move with an effortless motion,
running to You across what feels like a relentless ocean.
Pounding waves tend to move me off the course,
that You have laid out for me;
yet Your love and strength will lead me on to victory.
Along this journey I will certainly fall and stumble,
but through it all, You supply the much-needed grace,
to keep me humble.
In my limited sight and wisdom, I cannot see where You are leading me,
but I have enough faith in Your word,
to hold on and see what the end is going to be.
I press toward the goal of one day seeing You face to face,
while praying that You continue to hold me in the grip of Your grace.
Neither am I perfect not have I always been kind,
but I know that Your word tells me that of I knock,
the door will be opened and if I seek, I will find!

God's Promises

Sometimes in life we are thrown lots of curves,
some expected, some we never see coming.

As in all things, we should always lift our eyes, open our minds,
humble our hearts, and pray without ceasing that whatever comes our way,
God will grant us a peace that surpasses all understanding.

Living life is not an easy task but looking at the world
through the eyes of Christ should allow us to step back
and re-evaluate our priorities to know that the life we are given
is sometimes not the life we would have chosen if we had been given
a choice.

God never promised that the roads we must travel would be smooth ones,
but He did promise that He would be with us on our journey until we
reach our destination.

If heaven is your goal, try then to live life as Christ did, if not,
live like you always have and offer no excuses.
In short, live simply, love generously, care deeply, speak kindly
and leave the rest to God!

Everlasting Love

I have loved you with an everlasting love and have never forsaken you.
You are flesh of My flesh, bone of My bone, My most precious creation.
You were wonderfully and fearfully made in My image.
I molded you into the perfect creature that you are for many reasons.

I want you to face adversity and learn to overcome it.
I long for you to look at the world through My eyes and realize what it took for me to know that I would have to bleed and die for your sins and still be rejected.
I want you to know that I am the One who tends to all your needs, no matter how big or small.

If you knew the love that I have for you in My heart, would you come away from the clamor of this world and give yourself to Me?

Your Provider

I hear your voice; I see your tears.
I am Jesus; I am always here.
Cast all your cares and worries at my feet;
I am your provider, and never will you have to worry,
about what to wear or what you will eat.
You were set apart, long before you were ever born,
into this cruel and antagonistic world,
I see you as my greatest creation,
nonetheless you being a boy or a girl.
My love for you runs deeper than your fears
and there is nothing that you will ever go through,
that will tempt me to leave your side.
Because you are My child, My chosen one, who gave Me your heart,
neither the gates of hell nor the devil within it will ever be able to reside.

What Hatred Cannot Do

Hatred cannot stop someone from loving you if they truly loved you from the start.
Hatred cannot stop the birds of the air form singing a heavenly some each morning.
Hatred cannot stop a soul from being saved.
Hatred cannot prevent a Christian from being g witness to the goodness of God.
Hatred cannot break your spirit if you are rooted in Christ.
Hatred cannot alter God's plans for tour life.
Hatred cannot corrode the peace that comes only from God.
Hatred cannot kill true friendships.
Hatred cannot destroy self-confidence.
Hatred can NEVER minimize the power of the Resurrection of Jesus Christ!

Turned Upside Down

It is not often that we receive a heads-up that catastrophe is on the way,
because we are clueless to what awaits us from day to day.
Believing in the omnipotent God when we face trials means
that there is nothing more we need to say,
because faith in our Creator will give us the strength to stay.
We tend to fret about things that we have no control over,
yet conveniently forget that the God we serve is the Great Jehovah.
No matter what befalls us from one day to the next,
we must have faith that God knows what is best.
All that we own can be taken away in an instant,
yet none of that matters when we stand,
hand in hand with God and be consistent.
God will take our world that has been turned upside down and set it right again,
because He is God, from beginning to end!

True North

If I go left, You are there waiting to pull me back to You.
When I venture out into my wilderness of humanity,
to chase the world's offerings,
You are right there with out-stretched arms,
waiting for me to embrace You once again.
When my way leads me down a path to nowhere,
You gently invite me to try it Your way.
My moral compass is not always correct,
but Yours is never broken and will forever point me
in the right direction.
Good or bad, right, or wrong, no matter what I do,
You are my true north that always leads me back to You.

Touched By Life

We come into this world, innocent, yet sinful by nature, loving, yet prone to hate. As we experience love and the heartbreak that it can sometimes bring, we can attest to being touched by life.

When we suffer heartbreaking setbacks and experience monumental losses, we can attest to being touched by life.

God is not the choreographer of calamity in our lives, but He does orchestrate a positive outcome of it to allow the watching world to know that He is the Son of God and is able to take the bad and turn it into something good, to take the negative and turn it into something positive, that we would never dream could be possible.

For true believers, we have faith that with God, all things are possible, even the direst situations that our human minds cannot fathom could be used to be a blessing in our lives and to bring glory to God's holy name. Life will eventually touch us all, so it is vital that we tap into God's word, meditate on it, digest it, and share it with a dying, yet hungry world. It is imperative that we do our part, as Christians, to further the gospel of Jesus Christ and honor the Lord by sharing how we have been positively touched by life and by Jesus!

The Most Important Words

The most important words you will ever say to a friend are, "Thank you."

The most important words you will ever say to an enemy are, "I forgive you."

The most important words you will ever say to a child are, "I will protect you."

The most important words you will ever say to a parent are, "I love you."

The most important words you will ever say to yourself are, "I am worthy."

The most important words you will ever say to a lover are, "I am willing to trust."

The most important words you will ever say before God are, "I DO"

May your hearts and souls forever be bound together in love~

The Grip of Grace

Hold me steadfast in the grip of Your grace so that once my journey has ended,
I will see Your radiant face.
It is then I will know that my labor was not in vain,
even though my path to You was tedious and often laced with pain.
You kept me close to Your heart even when I did not deserve
Your unconditional mercy and grace,
yet Your loving kindness sustained me and held me safely in place.
I kneel boldly before Your throne of grace with gratefulness and gratitude,
while never forgetting Your precepts covering the Beatitudes.
True to the meaning of the word that you can wear proudly across your chest,
you are one of God's anointed, who is truly happy and blessed!

Standing on Faith

You are the hope that I cling to when the pressures of life
seem to weigh me down.
I hold to the hope that lies within me to stand on the faith
that renews me day by day.
Thank you for the unending love that was laid at my feet before my birth,
the kind of love that allows me to never be cast down
and to understand my worth.
Fill me with Your Holy Spirit and refresh my soul,
keep me mind, body, and spirit as You continue to make me whole.
Pull me closer when I am tempted to flee from Your presence
and make my own choices,
I know that apart from You anything that I listen to
will always be negative voices.
Allow me to run with endurance and finish this race,
as You lovingly hold me in the grip of Your amazing grace.

Slipping Away

Like a ship without a sail being tossed about the sea,
the faith that was once so strong appears to be failing me.
My thoughts that used to be centered around the word to sustain me,
are now scattered and distant, a mere shell of what they used to be.
My soul is nearing empty, bordering on becoming bankrupt,
and all that is within me is on the verge of becoming corrupt.
Oh, how I long for the close fellowship with You again,
to feel the newness of Your offerings to me so that new life can begin.
I feel Your presence without ever having to wonder if You are real,
because I know that You are the only One who can bring lasting peace
to my soul and allow me to heal.
Broken hearts never have to remain broken if they are given to You,
in love and submission, not just as a token.
You are a healer as well as a restorer,
a life held in Your hands will become richer even more.
Please do not allow me to slip so far away from You,
that Your heavenly kingdom is no longer within my view.
Hold me close and never let me go,
because Your face is what I long to see, this I know.

Show and Tell

Don't just tell Me that you love Me, show Me.
Don't just tell me that you appreciate me, show Me.
Don't just tell Me that you believe in Me, show Me.
Don't just tell Me that you trust that I have your back, show Me
Don't just tell Me that you want Me to be a part of your life, show Me.
Don't just tell me that you are with Me for the long haul, show me.
Don't just tell me that you believe that Jesus died on the cross for your sins,
show Me.
Don't just tell me that you believe that Jesus is the Son of the Living God, show Me.
Don't just tell me that you are saved and sanctified, show Me.
Don't just tell me what a difference Jesus has made in your life,
show Me.
Don't just tell Jesus that you know He lives… show Him!

Stop, Drop and Roll

Stop, drop and roll is a clever technique introduced by firefighters,
to help children learn the dangers of fire safety.
The technique is supposed to save your life by stopping where you are, dropping to the ground and rolling back and forth to extinguish the flames.
While "Stop, Drop and Roll" is useful for putting out fiery flames on clothing,
it doesn't work so well if you end up in hell.
If you want to go to Heaven and live for all eternity with God,
you simply need to:
STOP..... sinning and repent,
DROP.... bad habits and behaviors,
ROLL.... with Jesus and obey His commands.
What works on earth, does not work in heaven!!

Saving Grace

Forgive me for the wrong that I do,
that continuously moves me further away from You.
Let me not assume that since You are full of mercy and saving grace,
that You will not allow me to fall flat on my face.
When my thoughts, words and deeds do not align with Your will for my life,
there is no need to wonder why one situation after another fills me with strife.
My heart longs to be in total communion with You,
however, my sinful flesh and humanity seem to win the battle
for righteousness and vanity.
Like a ship being guided in from the stormy seas,
to the calm and gently shore,
I long to tap into Your peace,
where You will remember my sins no more.

Precious in His Sight

You are the hope that I cling to when
the pressures of life seem to weigh me down.
I hold on to the hope that lies within me
and stand on the faith that renews me day by day.
Thank you for the unending love that was laid out at my feet,
long before my birth,
it allows me to never be downcast or heavy-laden
and because of You, I know my worth.
Fill me with Your Holy Spirit and refresh my soul,
keep my, mind, body and spirit and make me whole.
Pull me close when I am tempted to flee from Your presence, and make my own choices,
apart from You, anything I listen to will only be negative voices.
Let me run with endurance and finish this race,
as You continue to hold me in the grip of Your amazing grace.

Praising You

Praising You during the troubled times,
meant that there were peaceful times to come.

Praising You during the times I was talked about,
meant that there were loyal friends to come my way.

Praising You when my rent was past due,
meant that there was a financial blessing waiting just around the corner.

Praising You when my boss seemed to be more of an enemy than a confidant,
meant that there was a better job waiting for me.

Praising You when everything that could go wrong did go wrong,
meant that easier times were just ahead just waiting for me to embrace it.

Peace

Quiet my mind, that races from one thought to another and let me find rest,
blanket my soul from the cares of the world so that I may pass the test.
My will is to pray for Your will to be done in my life,
allow me to lay aside all jealousy, malice, and strife.
Pour into my spirit, Your life saving love, until I no longer feel empty and confused.
Let me show compassionate love to all and offer no excuses.
Smooth out the rough places in my life,
bring about a calmness that cannot be explained,
love me, as a nursing mother with her child,
with an excitement that cannot be contained.
Despite my wrongdoings and devilish endeavors,
that pull me farther away from You,
keep me close to Your heart and give me peace,
to do what You have commanded me to do.
Let me love others, just like You told me to do,
allow the world to know that I can only love this way,
because of You.

My Prayer for You

My prayer for you is that when your eyesight begins to fade,
and your footsteps become slower and less urgent,
that you will never forget that God is the God of the here and now,
just as He was the God of your youth.
My prayer for you is that during trying times you will allow God to take away,
any ill-spirited rants and ravings and replace them with songs of Zion.
My prayer for you is that God will give you a new song to sing when there is no joy in your heart,
and that you will always remember to be slow to anger but quick to show others that you care.
My prayer for you is that when you look back on past trials and heartbreaks,
you will count it all joy for allowing God to close one door in order to open another.
My prayer for you is that you will always remember that His grace and mercy
is more than enough for you to carry out the plans that He has laid for you.

It Could Have Been Me

It could have been me, being able to identify with parents
who lost their child and will never be able to hold them in their arms again.
It could have been me, being able to identify with a devastated spouse
who was blindsided by the end of a marriage,
by a spouse who walked out on the family altogether
to chase what the world had to offer.
It could have been me, being able to identify with the worker
who lost the only job that provided for their family.
It could have been me, being able to identify with the patient
who was diagnosed with a life ending disease,
that did not leave much hope of survival.
It could have been me, being able to identify with the person
who could not cope with the everyday issues that life threw their way
and turned to drugs and alcohol to cope
but later found out that the very mechanism they used to cope
made the situation worse.
Life happens to us all and it could have been me,
but by the grace of God, He stepped into my life and made me brand new,
from the inside out.
No matter what issues we face in life,
we have the assurance that God is always by our side,
to shield and protect us from all hurt, harm and danger.
God never promised a life free from pain and suffering,
but He did give us His Holy Spirit to comfort us amid it all.
Trust God through it all!

If

If I could go back to yesterday and right the wrongs that I have done today,
I would jump at the chance to allow God to have His way.
If I could undo the tangled thoughts that travel through my mind
and eventually become habits,
I would save myself a lot of heartache and unnecessary havoc.
If I could go back to being a child and listen more intently
to what my parents had to say,
I would relish those moments in time and allow it to guide me in a better way.
If I could go back to the day before we met and rewrite our love story,
would I, or would I see us for who we are now and give God the glory?
If I had the chance, one last time, to hold my mother's out-stretched hand,
would I let go of that chance in hopes that she would understand?
If I could turn back the hands of time and recreate my history,
would I be smart enough to understand that God has already written my destiny?

I Choose You

Let my thought process always reflect Your heart,
one that is pure and true.
Thine sovereign and holy nature abides
within the innermost places of my being.
In You I find strength to forge ahead
when my life seems to spin out of control.
My life, my soul and my mind are the most precious fragments
that You so graciously hold.
Renew a right spirit in me so that when I lose my way,
I will not forget that it is You,
who binds me to Your side every day.
Draw me near to Your sanctified pavilion,
as I endure test after earthly test,
where my battered soul may find,
its much needed and welcomed rest.
Forsake me not when I lose my way,
but always remember me, no matter how long I remain astray.
My life is in Your hands, unto You I lift my voice,
hold me in the hollow of Your nail scarred hands
as I continue life's journey,
for I will forever be faced with a choice.
I choose You, Lord!

I Am Enough

I am enough of a child to know that no matter what happens in this world,
my parents will always protect me.
I am enough of a friend to know when someone needs a listening ear or a shoulder to cry on
and be able to respond accordingly.
I am enough of a daughter to know that I am a direct reflection of my parents,
and that my actions are a direct reflection of my upbringing.
I am enough of a woman to know my worth,
and to know that I am worthy of giving love and receiving it.
I am enough of a sister to give to my siblings the kind of love that I expect to get from them.
I am enough of a wife to share my heart, unconditionally,
with my spouse and trust that he will guard it with his very life.
I am enough of a believer to fear the Lord and bless His name.
I am enough of a Christian to share God's word and show kindness to others,
without expecting anything in return.
For anyone who has ever felt the pain of rejection, despair of loss or hurt,
remember that God loves you and will be with you, even in the lowest places.
He is ready to elevate you, but do not expect God to move on your behalf,
if you are not willing to move your feet!

God's Word

God's word sustains us when loneliness, despair, and doubt creeps in,
attempting to steal the joy that the Master says is ours.
God's word rebukes us when we get off the beaten path of righteousness
and allow our internal and fleshly compass to be our guide.
God's word guides us when we get lost in our wilderness of confusion,
wants, hopes,
and earthly ambitions, and points us back to Him.
God's word comforts us when life is lost on this side of heaven,
for we as Christians understand that this side is not the end.
God's word must be meditated on in our heart, mind, and spirit,
while soaring to new heights in seeking wisdom, knowledge and
understanding of the Creator of heaven, earth, and all things within.
God's word must be understood from both earthly and heavenly
perspectives to be effective.

Down on My Knees

Down on my knees is where I can find rest for my weary soul;
down on my knees is how my broken spirit is made whole.
Down on my knees is where I have the most intimate conversations
with the Highest God;
down on my knees is the position I take whenever life gets too hard.
Down on my knees is where I go,
when family and friends become my enemy;
down on my knees is what I must do
to discern what God has in store for me.
Down on my knees is where you will find me as I meditate
on God's unadulterated word;
down on my knees is the safe haven
where I know my prayers will be heard.

Choices

When I am faced with the choice to do right or to do wrong,
Lord, please allow me to always choose to do what is pleasing
in Your sight over fulfilling the pleasures of the flesh.
When I am faced with the choice to do good or to do bad,
Lord, please let me always choose to do Your will
over the urgings of my peers.
When I am faced with the choice to spitefully do harm to another or
uplift them,
Lord, please allow me to choose forgiveness over revenge.
When I am faced with bigotry and discrimination,
Lord, allow me to always choose love over hate.
When I am faced with the choice to stand in the gap for someone
or to be self-serving,
Lord, please allow me to choose prayer over my own desires.
When I am faced with the choice to rub a victory in someone's face
or hold true to who you have called me to be,
Lord, please allow me to choose humility over arrogance.
When I am faced with the choice to choose life or death,
Lord, please allow me to choose You
and the everlasting love that you offer over what this world has to offer.

Can You Hear Me?

Can You hear me crying out for help?
Can You hear the cries of my wounded heart?
Can You hear the sound of my heart breaking?
Can You hear the footsteps of my adversaries?
Can You hear my plea for mercy?
Can You hear the desperation in my prayers?
Can You hear the silence of my groaning?
Can You hear me from on high as you witness my trials?
Can You hear me when I lie down and ask You to protect me through the night?
Can You hear me as I wake and give thanks for the morning light?
Can You hear me as I pray to You and make my petition for You to order my steps today?
Can You hear me Lord, I have so much to say!

Be with Me

I long to be reborn and start over again.
Not born of a woman but to be wrapped up
in Your sovereign and holy reign.
Let Your spirit engulf my soul.
All while holding me close to You,
making me whole.
In this life, trials and heartaches will come.
Through it all, we pray that Your will be done.
I strive to live a life that is pleasing in Your sight,
oh Lord, give me the ability to sidestep doing wrong
when it is so easy to do what is right.
Allow my life to be a testimony of Your mercy
and often undeserved grace,
until I stand before You, face to face.

A Plea for Mercy

Lord, please take away the pain that has taken up residency within my heart;
replace it with Your unspeakable joy.
I long for peace and a sense of normalcy that has been replaced
by doubt and confusion.
Forgive me for taking for granted that which you have given me
to love, honor and cherish.
Lord, grant me the power and authority to take back what was taken
from me,
because when I look around at the once familiar things in life,
it all seems jaded and suddenly unfamiliar.
My soul cries out to You, pleading for Your grace and mercy.
The tangled thoughts that flow through my mind,
the tears that stain my pillow and the heaviness in my soul
can only be lifted by Your immeasurable grace and ever sufficient mercy.
As good and evil battle for control over my soul, and even my life,
the joy of knowing You allows me to know that no matter how many times
You bring me to my knees in prayer,
my plea for mercy will never fall on deaf ears.
When no one else seems to care, it is comforting to know
that You are a God who understands my pain, fears, and insecurities.
I lift my hands and simply say thank you for Your mercy!

A Living Sacrifice

Your death produced life for me,
so allow my life to become a living sacrifice for You.
Willingly, I strive to present myself holy and undefiled to You,
because apart from You, it is impossible to be to thine own self true.
It matters not how many times You bring me to my knees;
I know that You will take care of me and provide for me as You please.
I cling to the hope that lies within me, given by Your divine power,
because Your grave and mercy sustains me, hour by precious hour.

A Grateful Heart

My eyes opened early this morning and I was able to see,
the new and tender mercies that You laid out for me.
My ears respond to the sound of the melody of the sweet song
being sung by the birds as they sat contently in the trees.
This sight and sound were more than enough to being me to my knees.
I purposely take the time, each morning,
to spend a few precious moments in prayer
and silent conversation with You, as I do every day,
yet this morning turned out to be a defining moment,
because it recalled the things I prayed about,
and the things You had to say.
I am ever grateful that You cleaned me up from the inside out,
and put a new song in my heart, by this simple act of love from You,
it tells me that I am set apart.
I now have a greater appreciation for things and people around me,
now that I have tapped into Your love,
so to You be honor and glory,
because this love and appreciation could only come from above.

A Giving God

I gave you free will to serve or deny Me,
yet you choose to follow your own selfish desires.
I gave you a world to inhabit, yet you choose to destroy it.
I gave you friends to interact with, yet you choose to back stab them.
I gave you beautiful homes to live in, yet you choose not to offer shelter
to someone in need of a bed to sleep in.
I gave you expensive cars to drive, yet you choose not to offer someone
a ride.
I gave you a Savior to take away the sins of the world,
yet you chose to crucify Him because you didn't understand
who He was or Who sent Him.
How much more must I give to you to have you turn your face to Me,
repent and be grateful for your many blessings?

Without My Permission

You took what was rightfully mine and used it for your lustful pleasure,
something that was innocent, precious and my most priceless treasure.
The fear, pain, and indescribable terror that you inflicted on me,
was almost too much to bear, but if your sinful desires were fulfilled
none of that mattered to you because you just didn't care.
Who would believe the story I had to tell,
the truthful one about the night you put me through hell?
Why would anyone think that you would stoop so low overpower a young,
innocent girl, who had no advocate on her side to prevent the crumbling
of her world.
You moved on as if nothing ever happened, aimlessly drifting through life,
being tossed, and driven like the waves of the sea,
never giving much thought to the horrible thing that you forced upon me.
My life is wonderful these days, by God's amazing grace.
Through prayer and faith, it is my hope that you will find your space.
The space that will lift you up, turn your life around
and prompt you to cry out for God's saving grace,
while He can still be found.
As Christ has forgiven me, I made the choice long ago to forgive you,
because I realized that you no longer hold any power over my mind,
body or soul, so I did what I had to do!
I choose to move forward in the light of the Lord
because I know that His word will not return to Him void!
I am healed and I am whole!

War is Hell

A simple word of thanks will never be enough,
to let you know how grateful I am for your unselfish
and unwavering acts of heroism and valor to your country.
Running into the arms of danger, without hesitation,
and wrestling with thoughts of home and family,
amid love of freedom is the fuel that propelled you to never give up.
Your eyes saw its fair share of despair and the unthinkable,
while your ears heard fear, sorrow, determination, and the will to live.
Your heart still bleeds for those who left and never returned,
as it always will.
Your mind is safely at home, yet somehow,
it is still on the battlefield, yearning to right the wrongs,
wondering if it will ever be safe to let go and dream again.
For those who doubt the validity of your pain,
they will never be able to understand the full scope of the stories you tell-
If they had to walk a mile in your boots,
it is then they would understand that "WAR IS HELL!!"

Use Me Wisely

I have solved problems.
I have been the problem.
I have thought of others.
I have not cared about others at times.
I have learned new things.
I have memorized scriptures.
I have loved with reckless abandon.
I have forgotten what love feels like.
I have plotted revenge on those who have harmed me.
I have forgotten about those I have hurt.
I have practiced forgiveness.
I have forgotten how to hate.
I have forgotten who I am or what I used to be,
so be ever careful to take good care of me and use me wisely.
More than anything…I have realized how much You love me,
no matter what I have done.
Who am I you ask?
I am the mind that governs your thoughts, words, and actions!

True Lies

You presented yourself to be friendly to my face,
yet you scandalized my name from place to place.
I held our friendship in the highest regard,
yet you treated it like it was something so easy to discard.
It was in the cards that you and I would eventually meet,
but due to your inappropriate nature and gossiping ways,
I had no other choice but to walk away and shake the dust off my feet.
What I thought was real and true from the very start,
turned out to be a lesson in mortification and a deep stab wound,
through my naive and entrusting heart.
My eyes no longer see the person that I once thought you to be,
yet deep inside I should have heeded the warning signs
that flashed before me.
Many things you said about others as you stood in my presence,
should have shown me that your colors were not true,
but I was so drawn into your sick web of influence,
that I got lost in thinking that my real friend was you.
My interaction with you has opened my eyes,
to whom you are and what you are all about,
for now, I know that you are not my friend,
and I know this without a shadow of a doubt.

The Ties That Bind

Though time and distance may separate us,
the love we share will never allow either to keep us apart.
We grew up loving each other so fiercely and completely,
only to go out into the world and forge our own paths,
slowly allowing family bonds to loosen and regrettably sometimes die.
We once took the time to share one another's burdens,
and if someone meant you harm you always knew
you had someone to stand up for you,
because once upon a time we were tight like glue.
We fussed and fought until the bitter end but when all was said and done,
we each knew who we could truly call a friend.
Many links have been broken in our once close-knit family chain,
but we know that our earthly loss was heaven's gain.
Our hearts and souls are forever bounded in love,
for that kind of intimacy comes solely from up above.
How do we get back to where we used to be,
without carrying animosity and strife along for the ride?
We can start by allowing God's love to abide!

The Sinful Struggle

Take me by the hand and lift the burden of this sinful struggle,
that I fight each day.
No matter how hard I try to create a safe distance between me and my past,
there is always a stark and unadulterated reminder that there is no such thing
as a safe distance.
Bad intentions that were formed in my mind lead to bad company,
that I chose to befriend and allow to penetrate my decision-making,
that should have been my own from the start.
Knowing what I know now, I wish that I would have had the foresight,
to listen to my own heart.
Oh, how I wish I could go back in time and talk to my younger,
more innocent self and pass on the understanding that eluded me back then.
Would I then have made the same choices,
or would I have just created different ones?
The snares that once enslaved me often revisit my spirit
and let me know that this sinful struggle is far from over,
but I have faith that no matter how dark the days become,
I am never alone in my struggle!

The Measure of A Man

It is not how virile or smart he thinks he is;
the measure of a man is that he loves God
and how he presents that image to the world.
When life knocks him down,
the measure of a man is that he will always come up swinging,
refusing to be defeated.
When love walks out and leaves him brokenhearted,
the measure of a man is not to allow himself to be broken.
Because his childhood dreams never materialized,
the measure of a man is to dream new dreams and make them happen.
When he makes the choice to father children,
along the journey there will be many disappointments and missed opportunities,
but the measure of a man is to be there for his children, no matter what.
When life teaches his children about the harsh realities of the world,
the measure of a man is to have already instilled the values
of self-love and God's unconditional love in them.
The priorities of your life become the treasures that mold your hearts.
Do you measure up?

The Essence of You

Your grace, your class, your style.
Your presence, your wit, your smile.
You show yourself friendly to anyone in need,
you are known to all as a true friend indeed.
Your light shines brightly for all to see,
that God has graciously bestowed His blessings on thee.
You walk in His word and follow His commands;
never do you fail to lend a helping hand.
You delight in the ways of the Lord and ensure that we are all aware,
that God has been, is and always will be there.
It is not always easy to put on a brave face for the world to see,
yet you manage to do it with class and dignity.
Thank you for always being ever so kind,
for someone like you is a real treasure to find.
The Lord has blessed you with a long and fruitful life,
and to your husband you have been a blessing just by being his wife.

Technology

Android, iPhone, Samsung, LG,
all these brands have suddenly become
so interconnected to me.
I open my eyes and give thanks for another day,
then before you know it,
I am wondering where I left my tablet yesterday.
I play games, look up facts, stream music and watch TV shows,
then as I scroll down, I instantly become bombarded
with woe after woe.
So many things vie for our attention in this day and age,
from television, mobile phones, computers, and the like,
it is becoming increasingly difficult to discern wrong from right.
Images of things that do not serve an educational purpose
are thrown at us intentionally,
after a while it tends to border on duplicity.
For our children's sake and that of our own,
we must conquer the technology demon,
so that the hold will not blanket the next generation,
when they are grown.
Are you a slave to technology?

Silent Cries

A whisper, barely audible, crying out to be heard.
A subtle plea, crying out for the pain to subside.
Suffering through silent tears, yet never willing to be broken.

Despite unbearable circumstances and indescribable humiliation,
when no one wanted to be responsible for my pain,
God's still, small voice echoed through to remind me that He was still
in control.

Not knowing who to trust after being the object of his filthy lust,
silently, I prayed to die so that no one would have the chance
to judge me for an act that was not my own doing.

Silently, I longed to be held in my mother's warm embrace
and to see a look of understanding on my father's face.
It never came, no matter how hard I tried. Still, silently I prayed to die.

Silently I prayed to die because I never thought I would come to know
the kind of pain that was forced upon me.

Silently I prayed to be made whole, yet knowing
that all innocence was forever lost, so silently I prayed to die.

Silently I prayed for justice and closure from those
who promised to always protect me, but it never came.

As the years passed, silently I prayed for the strength to accept my fate
and move past the pain and not give in to the hatred
that had settled into my being, not knowing if I ever could.

Still, silently I prayed to be released from the mental prison
I had been locked in for so long… and still I pray~

Remember When?

Brilliance of mind, coupled with unmatched wit,
those qualities were once my friend before I started to forget.
Ever so quick with the quips and comebacks,
never at a loss for words or finding something to say.
Suddenly, I find myself searching for the right words
that used to come naturally, just yesterday.

Once upon a time I was able to think quickly and effortlessly,
now what was once considered child's play,
has given way to an unending struggle for normalcy.
Solving problems, mine, or someone else's,
was once second nature to me, but has strangely become
a ball of confusion that has given me cause to worry.

Jumbled thoughts, along with uneasy conversations,
now have a stronghold on me mentally,
and have taken hostage the once brilliant mind that solved problems,
loved fiercely, pondered life's greatest mysteries.
Now here I stand, looking in the mirror at this person
I used to know so well,
but as that person stares back at me,
I suddenly realized that I no longer have a story to tell.

Reflections of A Wife

I spent so much time doing the necessary things it took for us to build a life,
it seems I never really took the time to figure out if I was being a good wife.
I tried to cook, clean, and tidy up our home but looking back I realize
there may have been times when you may have felt neglected and left
all alone.
It was my goal to always be the mate you wanted and needed me to be,
yet I am certain I fell short at times, by just being me.

My love for you has always been genuine,
even when you needed so much more than I could give you,
other than my time.
As I reflect on days gone by,
my frequent shortcomings often bring a tear to my eye.
I love you in and out of time and space and wherever you are,
if we are together, I am certain I am in my rightful place.

Picking Up The Pieces

This morning started out as normal as I expected it to be,
yet as the day went on, I had no clue of what was waiting for me.
The clouds rolled in and suddenly everyone started to panic,
because what started out as a calm and easy day,
instantly turned frantic.

Minds racing and hearts pounding,
the calmness of the moment turned into despair,
because we were being instructed that we should not be here.
The race was on to get away as quickly as we possibly could,
because getting to safety was for our good.
The road that laid before us would not be an easy one to take,
and neither was it painless to fathom the devastation
that would lie in its wake.

We were left with no choice other than to leave,
and find a safe resting place,
we moved swiftly and methodically,
as we made haste.
We waited and prayed,
not knowing when the storm would pass,
yet we held on to our faith,
that You are the First and the Last.

Through it all, You held us close and never let us go;
as we face difficult situations,
You are bigger than it all, because the bible tells us so.
Thank you for keeping us and holding us close to You;
for we know that nothing is allowed to touch us
unless You give it permission to!

Optimism

We must forget the mistakes of the past
and look forward to the promises of the future.
Be as enthusiastic about the success of others
as you are about your own.
Own up to your mistakes and learn from them;
rise to the challenge to never repeat them.

If a past love broke your heart,
remember that a broken heart does not mean a broken spirit.
Greet everyone with a smile and speak health, wealth, and prosperity,
while always being of good cheer.
Think of the best, work toward the best and only accept the best.

In stature, be too large to worry, too noble to anger, too strong to fear,
and too happy to allow the presence of trouble to steal your joy.
Be courageous in the face of adversity and uncertainty.
Spend more time improving yourself
and less time criticizing others.

Numb

Your love turned on me, cold as ice,
when it should have been the liquid that warmed my soul.
Instead of making me feel like the person you promised to keep safe,
love and protect, you forgot to have and to hold.

My senses have become accustomed to being dull and unresponsive,
to the point that I no longer crave your touch.
You have taken something out of me that cannot be replaced,
and right now, it just doesn't hurt as much.

I am tired, lonely, and feel completely rejected,
yet there is a renewed sense of energy within me that needs to be ejected.
Once I gather what is left of my feelings and start moving on,
you will see how determined I am to make it on my own.

Love to My Father

If I could speak a word to your soul to keep you with me for all eternity,
I would simply hold you close and never let go.
Like sand in an hourglass, time will not wait for me to express to you
the gratitude my heart holds for you and how you have blessed my life.

From my beginning, you held my hand and guided me along this journey called life,
helping me to avoid many dangerous pitfalls, just through the words you spoke.
Rarely did you realize that what you said outweighed what you did,
even when you meant it as a joke.

If I could have you with me forever, that would not be long enough;
but if I could speak a word to your soul to keep you with me for all eternity…
that word would simply be STAY!

Life Stories

Tell me who you are as best you can,
it is my deepest desire to get to know you
from when you were a child and now that you are a man.

Share with me the details of your past, so that I will fully understand
what it took for you to make peace with your life.
Your blood courses through my veins and floods me with part of your identity,
therefore, it could be to my advantage or my worst enemy.

Whatever the reasons for the choices you had to make,
please know that my curiosity stands in your wake.
I envision the nuances that evolved into the love affair that eventually led you
to take the love of your life to become your wife.

Kindness is but one of the wonderful gifts you have shown
throughout your life, as you have remained strong,
for the sake of your children, as well as your wife.

Again, tell me who you are as best you can,
it is my deepest desire to get to know you
from when you were a child and now that you are a man.

I Am Tired

I am tired of allowing my flesh to control my thoughts and actions
because it continues to move me away from You.
I am tired of listening to the negative chatter of so-called friends,
who have no regard for Your word like I do.

I am tired of feeling unworthy of the love that I truly deserve,
to say the least, they have got some nerve!
I am tired of settling for whatever people try to give me
that is not worthy of my time or energy.

I am tired of having the good, bad, and ugly episodes of our existence,
being called back to my memory.
I am tired of going through the motions
and oftentimes thinking that I do not have a choice.

I am tired of feeling like I do not matter
and always being looked at as just another angry black woman,
who does not know how to use her God-given voice.

Now that I am tired of being tired,
it is time for me to do something about it.
Get out of my way and watch as I blaze a trail,
because I am too determined to quit!

From The Inside Out

I am so broken, from the inside out,
that I sometimes do not want to pray.
It is not that I have forgotten about Your goodness,
it is just that I do not know what to say.

My heart is so heavy at times and my burdens seem almost unbearable,
so the only thing that feels right to my soul,
is to fall on bended knee and cry out to You!

When my burdens get too heavy and seem to weigh me down,
Your strength lifts me up and Your grace and mercy always abounds.

You put a song in my heart even when there is no smile on my face.
Hiding myself in Your pavilion, to spend sacred time in Your presence,
is my only safe resting place.

I am so broken, from the inside out, that my soul feels empty and confused, but Lord, I thank You for Your strength and grace that allows me to be renewed.

Facets of Depression

What is this thing that keeps hanging over me,
whatever it is, it won't let me be.

My body and soul cry out for relief,
but in its place, all I find is anguish and grief.

In my state of grief, it seems the even though prayers go up,
blessing never seem to come down,
in my attempts to ease my pain,

I continue to search for God while He can still be found.
Even in the silence, God is working things out for my good;
how do I know, because the word said that He would.

Whatever this thing is that just won't let me be,
I must continue to fight it with everything I have inside of me.
Just when I think I have it beat and can finally see the light,
it eventually comes back at me and so begins yet another fight.

I continue to pray for the strength that I know will one day come,
until then I keep on fighting until my battle is won.

Coronavirus Blues

Don't let the coronavirus get you down because we are believers and, in our house, it will not be found.
Keep trusting in God to see you through,
He will do exactly what He said He would do.
God did not give us a spirit of fear but one of love,
power, and a sound mind.
Boldly seek His face and ask what you will of the Savior,
because His word declares that if you seek, you will find!

Bent But Not Broken

My heart aches and cries out for mercy that I do not deserve,
because my wrongdoings have taken me to a place of unbelievable despair.

You seem to be a million miles away from me,
but I know in my heart that is not true,
for You are a God of decency and order and You always come through.
My mind, my heart and my soul are being bent to their limits,
but You continue to hold me in the hollow of Your hand,
and I refuse to allow myself to be broken.

If it was possible to press "rewind" to make the pain stop, I would do it,
but since that is not possible, all I can do is go through it.

I have to own the mess that I have created and trust Your process
to get me through because in the midst of all of the pain, heartache
and devastation I was a part of, I know that the only thing I can do is
look above.

Nothing can ever be said that will take away what has been done,
but it is my prayer that in time You will restore marriages, friendships
and give us the hope that the victory will be won.

Nothing will ever be the same, as it was before,
and looking ahead, a tough and tedious battle is in store.
I am ready to reclaim my place as Your child for now I know, with all certainty,
that You never moved away from me, it was me who moved away from You,
one dangerous step at a time.

While I wasted precious time trying to chase the offerings of the world,
I never stopped to realize that I had the world with me from the start,
Then again, no one ever said that I was smart!

I humbly ask for Your forgiveness and the forgiveness of those I have hurt along the way.
Whether this forgiveness will ever come my way, I do not know
but I must continue to trust Your process
and accept the love that You have for me as a token,
for at this very moment, I remain bent, but by Your grace, not broken.

Acceptance

There is a smile on your face for the whole world to see,
but the story is quite different when it is just you and me.

No matter how strong and agile you try to be,
there is a hold that has you so tightly bound that it seems impossible
for you to break free.

Where you are now is a direct result of where you have been,
and only you and God know what you had to endure to get through
your journey.

Now that you are no longer in harm's way, physically,
you continue fighting the unseen enemy that refuses to let go of your mind.

It plagues you relentlessly to the point of distraction,
until it feels like all hope is lost,
but there is hope at the end of the darkest tunnel,
that comes at no cost.

Accept who you are and all it took for you to become this person,
and trust that our sovereign God is incapable of making mistakes.

The Word tells you that pride comes before your downfall,
but God is patiently waiting for you to place your complete trust in Him,
and surrender it all.

A Purposeful Birth

Many events took place long before your existence was ordained to be,
little did you know, you were fashioned to come into this world to give God the glory.

Setbacks and setups were oftentimes interlaced with your story
along your journey through life, yet you took the good with the bad,
the ups with the downs, along with heartaches and strife.

Many lessons were taught and learned on your tedious path,
some your parents could never teach you,
for many were life lessons that would eventually suck the life out of you then,
by design, would turn around and breathe into you a new life,
and make you brand-new.
Your journey has taken you to heights unknown
and landed you exactly where you were meant to be,
so take it all in stride and be happy with who you look in the mirror and see.

God has blessed you to celebrate all your years,
some have been loads of fun and laughter while some offered you unpleasant tears.
If your parents could see the man that you have become,
it would erase all their, then, doubts, worries, and fears.

Your life was crafted with a loving purpose in mind,
yet to understand the true meaning of that purpose is yours to find.

Enjoy your birthday, have your cake, and eat it too,
because today is yours to do with it what you want to.
Your parents would swell with pride at the man they labored for,
and saw the work of God when He gave you a purposeful birth.

A Blessing Born Out of Adversity

I never imagined that my deepest pain would one day
evolve into my sincere passion.
Something that was so brutal and tragic would, in some way,
be a life changing fashion.

Remembering it as if it happened yesterday,
yet longing to cast if from my memory,
trying to push it a million miles away.

There is not a day that goes by that does not bring on a trigger
that takes me back to that particular time and place,
but lucky for me, I have been a witness to God's amazing grace.

To look at me and get to know the true essence of who you see,
I am a woman who God held securely in His hands,
when He allowed my blessing to be born out of adversity.

Will You Think of Me?

When the time comes, and I cease to be;
tell me how often will you think of me?

The love we shared, the laughter we had;
we truly loved each other, even when we were mad.

You loved me with a fierceness that rocked my world,
because you always showed me that for you,
I was your one and only girl.

The storms we weathered were just a very small part of our story,
yet through our ups and downs and times of uncertainty,
God kept us together and to Him be the glory.

He held us in the grip of His amazing grace from our youthful day,
until this present moment in time.
He had a purposeful plan for our lives that we could not understand,
because it had no reason or rhyme.

When My Life Is Over

When my life on earth is over, Lord please let it have been worthwhile,
so that I will not be remembered only for my failures and mistakes.

I have been kissed on the lips by ambition and courted by the trappings
that the world had to offer, yet none of that matters,
for where I aim to be is with the Father, the Son
and the Holy Spirit, embracing me so lovingly.

During my life there have been many ups and downs,
coupled with many heartaches, yet through it all,
You kept me and never let me down,
once I accepted Your gift of salvation, You turned everything around.

Neither am I perfect, nor have I always been kind,
but I pray that You will not allow my mistakes to bind me to the past,
that I have tried so hard to make amends for.

You gave new life to my thoughts, a new rhythm to my walk,
and a new attitude to how I treated others.
How happy will I be when I see Your face,
because all I want to see are beautiful things surrounding me.

Your tender mercy and loving kindness have been the mechanisms
that propelled me through the storms of life,
when they threatened to overtake me.

Heaven is my goal and to hear You say,
"Well done, my good and faithful servant",
will be the crown for which I have labored for all along.

The Whisper

Where are you when I need you to hold me tight?

Where are you when I need reassurance,
that everything is going to be all right?

Where are you when the nights are cold and lonely?

I feel lost and alone without you near,
I need you close to help erase all my fears.

Where are you now that I need help trying to figure this all out?

I was told that for you, "there is no more sorrow,
no more pain because your earthly suffering,
was for heaven's gain"

You see, Jesus whispered in my ear and told me,
that you are safe from all harm, now that you are
resting in His arms.

Continue to love me as I still love you,
until we meet again!

Take Your Rest

Time has come and gone, and I struggle to understand,
how God's Word will sustain me through my grief
because the pain of loss is so great and the emptiness in my heart is real.

Every day I wake up I put my entire being on autopilot
and go about my day. I must keep myself and my mind occupied
so that I do not think about the emptiness
that was once filled with the wholeness of love,
laughter, and a sense of feeling needed.

Nothing has been right in my world since your transition,
as I struggle to remember the joy that was once my constant companion.
Now it all seems like a distant memory, that has been foreshadowed by
what once was.

I long to be in the space and time of being your mother,
friend, and confidant.
I cherished holding hands, sharing secrets,
and often just sitting in silence with you,
enjoying our little corner of the world.

Those memories have sustained me in my darkest hours.
Now that you are only with me in spirit,
I hold on to the promise that soon we will be reunited,
and all will once again be right in my world.
Wait for me and when it is time, I will smile and greet you with open arms!

Until then, take your rest…

Season of Grief

What can be done with the grief that engulfs my soul,
and stains my pillow at night?
I cry out to You in hopes of finding the much-needed relief
that I long for during this season of grief.

My soul is an empty vessel that was once filled
with an exuberant and unexplained joy,
but now the cracks and crevices have given way to an emptiness,
that can only be filled with the warmth of Your embrace.

Hold me in the hollow of Your nail scarred hands,
and gently guide me back to You.

How my soul yearns for the opportunity to turn back the pages of time,
to go back to what used to be, yet it is not in Your will for me to do.

As I try to process the enormity of the test that will become my testimony,
be with me and allow me to "be still and know that You are God",
my one and only.

Room 301

The adversities you faced from birth, the uncertainty of your lineage,
the breakdown of your marriage, facing life as a single mother,
raising your children, worrying if you would instill the right values in them.

How you got to Room 301 is a mystery to us all, but faith tells us that
you will not be here forever. We look over and see your face,
so still and serene, it takes our breaths away.
We want to be inside your head to know what you are feeling
and what you are thinking as you lay so still in your bed.

We think back to years gone by when you gave us advice
on life, love, and things in general. I am sure you thought we were not listening,
but we listened with our ears, watched with our eyes and hid those
things away in our hearts.
While we did not fully understand the struggles you faced,
we knew that you did things that you otherwise would not have done
if it would have been only for your sake.

You did things that had no rhyme or reason, so we thought, but later came to know
that it was always for our good. The love you showed had a fierceness that rivaled
the best of mothers, to us, you were the best!!

Our reasons for wanting to keep you with us were selfish, and heart driven.
Once we realized that you had completed your journey and was ready to take your rest, we asked God to allow you to stay with us
"just a little while longer" but that was not to be.

At that point, our prayer was that God's will would be done in your life and that He would relieve you of the never-ending pain you endured, like only He could. Once we prayed that prayer,
that is when He said, "Well done, my good and faithful servant, welcome home!"

Reflections

I look in the mirror and the reflection that I see,
is a reflection of me, that is of you.

The resemblance is so striking that what I see, is a
reflect of you, staring back at me.

With a face so round and skin so smooth,
it must be you that I see in me.

The attitude is familiar because I embrace it like my own,
feisty, determined, and proud, not willing to be denied.
I was shaped in a way that was so lovingly inspired by you,
it sometimes overwhelms me to know that I reflect you and you reflect me.

I wear your reflection like a badge of honor,
and pray that I will do you justice by just being me,
while all the while being a direct reflection of you.

Missing You

We see your face even though you are no longer here.
We smell your scent even though you are no longer near.

You were our constant companion, never wanting to let us down.
Now that your time has come to say good-bye,
our happy hearted smile has been turned into a frown.

Thank you for being a wonderful mother and a faithful wife and friend,
please know that your memory will forever live in our hearts
until we all meet our end.

You held on and fought as long as possible,
but no matter how much we loved you,
God loved you best.

We miss you and mourn your passing,
for we know that you did not want to leave but had no choice.
We saw the pain and suffering you were enduring at the end
and knew that we needed to be your voice.

Rest in the arms of Jesus!

Letting Go

When it is time, we must let go…
We cherish the life and mourn the death
but know in our hearts that God knows best.

He never gives us more than we can bear,
so, we must trust that He is always there,
even during our pain, to comfort and carry us through.

The Lord gives us numbered days so we must give Him all the praise.
An easy life was not the promise that was given,
but following God's word will lead to a life that is purpose driven.

If you die in Christ, in sorrow or pain,
an earthly loss is heaven's gain.
Earthly vessels never want to let go,
but heavenly discernment will prompt us when it is time to do so.

When our time comes to rest safely with Jesus,
may the life we have led be an example to others
to follow Christ while they still have time.
For now, when it is time, we must let go…

I Can't Breathe

Today started out as normal as any other,
but never did I expect to be crying out for my deceased mother.

I left home expecting to return to my family and friends,
but what I did not know was that my life was about to end.
One indiscretion that did not have to define me,
allowed the whole world to see, up close and personal,
police brutality and the end of my dignity.

Human dignity is due to us all,
no matter what our background may be,
yet you still chose to kneel on my neck,
with the full force of your knee.

Your reckless actions left my loved ones utterly bereaved,
even though I told you repeatedly, "I Can't Breathe."

Fulfilling Your Destiny

When we met, I knew our love would last a lifetime.

We had so many plans: get married, raise a family,
and do the things that lovers do.

You made a vow to be my strength when I got weak,
and you fulfilled your destiny as a wife.

You made a vow to nurture our children in God's love
and you fulfilled your destiny as a mother.

All was well, even in trying times.
When real life confrontations caused our vows to break
you understood the true meaning of the word forgiveness
and made things right.

Although at times it seemed that I was too busy to slow down
and savor the little things that made our marriage special,
you still fulfilled your destiny by loving me
in spite of my faults and shortcomings.

What the world saw on the outside was not what you saw on the inside
and having you in my life, was, is and always will be
the reality of your destiny being fulfilled.

You fulfilled your destiny as a wife, mother, and child of God
and I am at peace knowing that you are resting with the Lord.

Forever in My Heart

I loved you with all my heart even before the beginning of time,
because I loved you before God ever made you mine.

When I first held you in my arms, time and space seemed to melt away,
the moment I looked into your eyes. It was in that instant when I realized
that God had truly blessed me with a priceless and beautiful surprise.

My hopes and dreams were wrapped up in your future
because I have never wanted anything but the best for your life,
happiness, joy, children of your own and of course a wife.

We did not always see eye to eye,
but you blessed my life in more ways than you will ever know,
and in this moment, I stand suspended, still not able to let you go.

Parenting does not come with instructions,
but I did the best I could for you from the start,
so no matter where you are or where I go,
you will always remain forever in my heart!

I Am, Because He Is

I am free to worship without fear of reprisal because He is the Bishop of souls.

I am worthy of love because He is my Advocate.

I am joyful because He is my Portion.

I am enlightened to the truth because He is an awesome Teacher.

I am full of hope for the future because He is a Wonderful Counselor.

I am never thirsty because He is the Living Water.

I am no longer inarticulate to the word because He is the Truth.

I am able to live in peace because He is the Prince of Peace.

I am no longer in darkness because He is the Light.

I am never hungry because He is the Bread of Life.

I am safe because He is my Shepherd.

I am who I am, because He is the Great, I am!

Love's Greatest Act

When Jesus came into being for the selfless act of dying on the cross,
in the place of billions of human beings who never do the same for Him,
that is when love's greatest act took place.

Jesus died for us without ever knowing our names,
He did it without a second thought of who would one day
come to love or reject Him.

God poured out His love when He sent down His one and only Son,
to die a horrific death for the sake of mankind.

Simply said, no other father would do this for someone they did not know,
and no other son would be willing to obey.

That was love's greatest act, in action!

Learn To Listen

I cried out to You as loudly as I could,
yet You remained silent.

I endured one heartache after another,
yet You remained silent.

I shedded sorrowful tears, praying that You would see them,
yet You remained silent.

I groaned out in painful agony with tears that bruised my very soul,
in anticipation of much needed relief,
yet You remained silent.

You called loved on after loved one home to rest,
I pleaded for acceptance and comfort,
yet You remained silent.

I struggled to hold on to my faith during troubling times,
yet You remained silent.

When I finally took the time to examine each situation You put me in,
that is when I realized the You were never silent,
I just never took the time to listen.

Senses

Our ears hear the senseless gossip being spoken unnecessarily about others,
while oftentimes missing God's intimate whisper,
telling us how much He loves us.

Our eyes see the injustice that plagues our society,
yet these are the same eyes that witness the miracle of birth,
and the wonders of God's amazing universe.

Our hands can be guilty of shedding innocent blood,
yet can be the same hands that touch the sick,
bringing healing to their bodies.

Our mouths can speak hateful words toward others,
yet will be the same mouth that will turn in an instant,
and give God praise. How can this be?

The parallels between right and wrong, good and evil,
should not be analogous, yet they are.

Our senses are infallible when we lean on God's strength,
and seek discernment in uncertain circumstances.

We Are Protected

God never told us that weapons would not form,
He said they would not prosper.

What God knows about us should be more important to us,
than what people think about us.

No one has the magic cure for life and the ills that come with it,
yet we do have a Savior who is bigger than it all.

We are protected by a God who is able to watch over the entire world,
yet be exclusive to us, all at the same time,
this speaks of His Omnipresence and deity as the Savior of the world.

We are protected by a God knows everything about each of us, better than we do,
this speaks of His Omniscience and His place as our Supreme Being.

We are protected by a God who is able to do anything He wants,
when He wants and to whom He chooses to do it to,
this speaks of His Omnipotence. He has maximal power at His disposal.

We are protected by a God of love, compassion, and forgiveness,
because His unconditional love shows compassion to us,
even when we do not deserve it.

He forgives our trespasses, time and time again and this lets us know that,
God's protection is more than enough,
each time we are faced with life's hardest quandaries.

Peaceful Existence

Lift me up and take me to another place,
one that has not been touched by sickness,
sorrow or pain.

Permit my mind to become a blank canvas,
so that it will bend to Your will
and accomplish what You want it to.

Allow my soul to levitate to a place of serenity,
that can only be supported by Your merciful hand.

Take my mind away to a hamlet of peace,
where only You and I are blended together as one,
in spirit and in truth.

Lead and I will follow,
speak and I will obey.

What Can We Render?

To what can we render unto God that He doesn't already own?
Our lives are under His rule, our steps have been ordered,
our hearts have been changed and,
our enemies have become our footstools.

He is a God of decency and order,
even though we go through seasons of hunger and fullness,
joy and pain, sickness and health,
He is with us, holding our hand and guiding us forward.

Whatever season we find ourselves in,
God is always there, delighting with us in times of plenty,
lamenting with us in times of emptiness.

He holds us close, as a mother holds her suckling child,
shielding us from harm, until our dark days have passed.

In times of plenty, give thanks,
in times of emptiness, pray without ceasing.

All we have belongs to God and He needs nothing from us,
except our commitment of faith to Him.
We cannot render anything unto God,
He already owns it all.

A Beautiful Surprise

To think that you even existed, just waiting in the wings for me,
was more than I could have ever imagined.
To have you materialize before my very eyes,
was more than I could ever have hoped for.
Yet here you are, a living, breathing and compassionate illustration
of an indulgent love that completes me.
Your touch blankets my mind, body, and soul, as if protecting me from the cold.
Your kisses are buttery soft like a breeze floating in the air
and the secure connection that is felt from my heart to yours
assures me that your presence is there.
When you whisper words of affirmation and shower me with the essence of you,
you put a joyful song within my entire being that no one can undo.
The reciprocity of affection and endearment that is shared between us is a joy to behold,
as it continues to pull me ever closer to you with an unabated force that is almost
impossible to be controlled.
Like the phoenix rising from the ashes to start anew,
so begins the beautiful love story of me and you!

TAKE ME AWAY

I want to throw all my worries to the wind, and let it take them far away from my mind.

I want to be the recipient of a love is so complete my heart will no longer recognize pain, hurt, or sorrow.

I want to engage in loving so mightily, that it will blanket my mate's soul, from his head down to his toes.

I want to go to a place where it becomes possible to touch the intangible, and hold on to it with all that I have within me.

I want to be in a space where the wind will carry my thoughts, to heights that are unfathomable to the human mind.

I want to be everything, while not having to be anything or anyone, all at the same time.

I want to listen without hearing negativity, while speaking edifying words of positivity.

I want to be moved outside of myself and permit my being to dissolve firmly, into Your existence so that I will be wrapped in Your circle of agape love, everlasting.

It's in the Blood

Bloodwork is the best way to reveal what is going on within our bodies.
Blood is a bond that ties family members together tighter than glue.
Sacrificial blood is relinquished on the battlefield as a debt of selfless gratitude for our freedom by our brave soldiers.
Innocent blood is spilled on the streets of our towns and cities every day because of gun violence.
There is one type of blood that has the power to save lives, offer forgiveness, change hearts and minds, and make you into a new creation.
This blood can only come from Jesus.
It was shed for the remission of our sins and gave us the right to petition God on our own behalf.
The blood of Jesus is like no other, and it can do abundantly more than anyone could imagine or comprehend.
The blood of Jesus is a perfect match to everyone's blood type, which makes us the perfect recipients to receive a blood transfusion of the heart, mind, and soul.
Jesus is A+ and A-..... Agape love
Jesus is B+ and B-....... Beloved Son of God.
Jesus is O+ and O-..... Omnipotent and Omnipresent.
It's in the blood!

Feelings

I know the feeling of falling in love with the right one
and praying that it will last forever.

I know the feeling of longing to start a family
and watch them grow up to be beautiful teenagers and responsible adults.

I know the feeling of laughing so hard at the "not so funny" jokes
until my stomach aches and loving every minute of it.

I know the feeling of looking into the eyes of my mate
and thinking that I am the luckiest person in the world.

I know the feeling of loving someone so much it hurts
and knowing that I never want that feeling to end.

I know the feeling of being loved unconditionally
and accepting that love with open arms and reciprocating that love.

I know the feeling of looking into the eyes of our children
and being amazed that I could love so deeply and so completely.

I know the feeling of experiencing a loss so deep
that it catches you by surprise and totally takes your breath away.

I know the feeling of being engulfed by loneliness, despair,
and a sense of overwhelming grief.

I know, all too well, the feeling of being safe in the arms of Jesus
and no matter the storm that rages around me,
I know that God is greater than my storm.

One thing I know for sure is that God is never the reason for my pain,
but that He is my comforter, and He will always be there
to see me through all of life's trials and tribulations.

About The Author

She started writing at the age of 13, as an escape while going through a trying period in her life. When she discovered that writing was cathartic, she stuck with it and continued to use it as an outlet to express herself. She has a bachelor's degree in Business Management and is currently working toward a master's in Criminal Justice. She is an avid animal lover of any kind!